FIRE SERVICE

COOKBOOK

VOL. 2

RECIPES FROM FIREFIGHTERS

WORKRITE FIRE SERVICE COOKBOOK VOLUME 2

Welcome to Workrite Uniform Company's second fire service cookbook — a celebration of the well-known fact that firefighters are every bit as impressive in the kitchen as they are on the job!

To all the master firefighting chefs who contributed to this cookbook, thank you for sharing your fantastic recipes. And, to all of the brave men and women in fire service, thank you for your commitment to protecting the communities you serve. It is an honor to see our flame-resistant (FR) station wear worn by such a remarkable group of individuals.

APPETIZERS & SIDE DISHES

Broccoli Salad

Misty's Southern Style Coleslaw

Sautéed Brussels Sprouts

Bacon Dip

BROCCOLI SALAD
David Fletcher - Texarkana Arkansas Fire Dept.

INGREDIENTS

1 bunch of broccoli (cut to bite size)

1 cup mayonnaise

⅓ cup sugar

2 tablespoons vinegar

1 cup mild cheddar cheese, grated

8 bacon slices cooked & crumbled

DIRECTIONS

Gently toss broccoli with bacon, set aside.

Mix the mayonnaise, sugar and vinegar in a small bowl.

Gently pour over broccoli/bacon and mix.

Stir in cheese, then refrigerate.

MISTY'S SOUTHERN STYLE COLESLAW

Misty Bearden - Alder Springs Volunteer Fire Dept.

INGREDIENTS

Two 10-ounce bags of Dole® Angel Hair Coleslaw or 1 large head of cabbage shredded fine.

1 medium to large Vidalia or sweet onion puréed. (It mixes and flavors better)

1½ tablespoons white vinegar

2 tablespoons sugar

½ teaspoon salt

½ teaspoon black pepper

¼ cup water

DIRECTIONS

Mix together ingredients for dressing.

Add cabbage and mix thoroughly.

Pat down evenly in bowl, cover and refrigerate for a minimum of 1 hour.

SAUTÉED BRUSSELS SPROUTS
Mike Jacobs - Healdsburg Fire Dept.

This is a delicious hearty recipe that can easily be adapted to accommodate vegetarian/vegan diets by leaving out the bacon. This is normally served as a side dish but could be an entrée by increasing the ingredients accordingly.

INGREDIENTS

Approximately 10 sprouts per person

1 strip of bacon per person

½ onion, diced

Garlic salt

Olive oil

Balsamic vinegar

Montreal® Seasoning

DIRECTIONS

De-stem the Brussels sprouts and cut into halves lengthwise. Place into Ziploc® bag and shake with balsamic vinegar, Montreal® Sasoning and garlic salt.

Finely dice onion.

Cut bacon into cubes.

Generously coat the bottom of the pan with olive oil. Place over medium-high heat, get oil hot but just below the point of smoking.

Add the bacon and cook until it just starts to crisp.

Add diced onions and cook until they just start to turn translucent (usually about 2 minutes).

Add the Brussels sprouts and stir to cook every couple of minutes.

Cook to desired level of caramelization/crispiness.

Season to taste and serve hot.

BACON DIP

Christopher Smith – Clay Volunteer Fire Dept.

INGREDIENTS

1 cup mayonnaise

1 cup sour cream

1 to 1½ pounds bacon, chopped

¼ cup onion, chopped (optional)

4 cups shredded sharp cheddar cheese

DIRECTIONS

Mix all ingredients together. This can be served immediately, but the flavors tend to get better after being refrigerated over night.

Garnish with chopped tomato and scallions, if desired.

Serve with chips, crackers or baguette.

SOUP / CHILI / STEWS

Ronnie's Gringo Chili Verde

Crockpot Sweet Chili

Historical Society Chili

Fire Brigade Potato Potage

Dustin's Award-Winning Chili

Taco Soup

Beef Stew

RONNIE'S GRINGO CHILI VERDE

Ronnie Gilman – San Miguel Fire and Rescue

INGREDIENTS

2 pounds top sirloin, tenderized

1 yellow onion, diced

4 cloves garlic, chopped

4 canned stewed Mexican tomatoes

4 canned diced Ortega® Green Chiles

¼ of remaining bacon drippings

1 cup seasoned flour

1 tablespoon cumin

DIRECTIONS

Cut sirloin into 1-inch by ½-inch pieces and dredge in seasoned flour.

Heat a cast iron Dutch oven or heavy pot and add bacon drippings.

Add sirloin and brown until meat has a good, brown coating.

Add onion and garlic and cook for 5 minutes.

Add Mexican stewed tomatoes and green chiles.

Season with cumin, salt, pepper and ground garlic to taste.

Cover and cook on low heat for approximately 1 hour or until meat is nice and tender.

Serve with flour tortillas.

Leftovers are also great the next morning with some fried eggs.

CROCKPOT SWEET CHILI
Janie Garringer - Susanville Fire Dept.

The appeal to this recipe is that you can leave it cooking all day, epecially during a busy shift or on a cold day. I cook it for our station's monthly dinner night when all active and past active volunteers come together.

INGREDIENTS

1 pound ground beef

5 cans of beans (light and dark kidney, black, pinto and northern)

1 can of corn

2 cups diced tomatoes

1 yellow onion, diced

1 orange bell pepper, diced

¼ cup brown sugar

2 tablespoons honey

1 packet of chili seasoning

*To add a little spice to your chili, add a diced jalapeño within the last two hours of cooking.

DIRECTIONS

Season and brown beef in a pan, set aside.

Open, drain and rinse all canned goods.

Dice all vegetables.

Put cooked ground beef and all vegetables into Crock-Pot and turn on low.

Add packet of chili seasoning, brown sugar and honey.

Mix everything together and cook on low for 6-8 hours.

Mix periodically throughout the day, add small amounts of water if needed to prevent drying out.

Enjoy topped with shredded cheese and cornbread.

Serves about 8. Recipe can be modified to serve more or less firefighters.

HISTORICAL SOCIETY CHILI
David Steinitz – Los Angeles City Fire Dept.

INGREDIENTS

2 cans of black beans or cannellini beans rinsed
(Feel free to use 3 cans if you like lots of beans)

1 cup of chopped mild fresh chiles (Use rubber
gloves and do not touch your eyes or go to the
bathroom with the gloves on)

2/3 cup chopped red onion

2/3 cup chopped celery

2/3 cup chopped red pepper

2/3 cup of white part of leek, washed well

2 garlic cloves, minced

2 tablespoons dried oregano

1 stick of unsalted butter

1/4 cup all purpose flour

4 cups of shredded cooked turkey or chicken
(or use cooked ground turkey or chicken as
desired)

4 cups of chicken broth (such as the low sodium
if possible, health you know)

2 1/4 cups of thawed frozen corn

2 tablespoons ground coriander seeds

2 1/2 tablespoons chili powder

4 tablespoons cumin

1/2 teaspoon salt

1/4 teaspoon sugar

Plain yogurt or sour cream (optional but
a good addition)

DIRECTIONS

In a pot cook the chiles, onion, celery,
bell pepper, leek, garlic and oregano in
butter over moderately low heat, stirring
occasionally for 10-15 minutes or until the
vegetables are softened.

Add the flour and the cooked turkey or
chicken and cook the mixture over low heat,
stirring for 15 - 20 minutes or until the flour is
golden.

Then stir in the chicken broth.

In a food processor, purée 1 1/2 cups of the
corn and then add the puree to the chili
with the remaining 1 cup of corn, coriander
seeds, chili powder, cumin, salt, sugar and
the beans.

Simmer the chili, stirring for 15 minutes.

As a bonus you can also put it all in a crock
pot on low for no more than 4 hours. It's nice
to serve out of in case you are doing a lot of
runs and like your food warm, if not hot.

Season the chili with salt and black pepper.

Serve with a dollop of yogurt or sour cream! I
add different hot sauces but only in my bowl
so as not to ruin the experience for everyone
else. I really like it hot.

Makes 6 small servings or 4 good bowls.

Ice cream for dessert and iced tea for the
beverage. A nice dark brew works best.

FIRE BRIGADE POTATO POTAGE

Joseph Gillipsie – Upper Township Fire Dept. Ohio

INGREDIENTS

1½ pounds Yukon Gold potatoes, peeled and diced

1 medium onion, diced

1 medium carrot, diced

1 stalk celery, diced

8-ounce pack of ham, diced

3 cloves garlic, sliced

3 tablespoons butter

¼ cup flour

4 cups chicken broth

2 cups water

½ cup heavy cream

Salt and pepper to taste

Cayenne pepper (optional)

Chopped fresh chives and/or shredded cheddar for garnish (optional)

DIRECTIONS

Melt butter in a stockpot over medium heat until golden brown. Stir in carrot, celery, onion, ham and garlic; cook and stir for 5-6 minutes, until the vegetables soften and the onions are tender.

Stir in flour and cook for about 3 minutes. Stir in chicken broth, 1 cup at a time. Add water and stir to combine. Turn the heat to high and bring to a simmer. Simmer on medium-low for 15 minutes, stirring occasionally.

Taste the soup for salt and add more if necessary. Stir in potatoes and cook for 15 minutes, until potatoes are tender.

With a potato masher, mash the soup a few times, leaving plenty of whole chunks of potato. Season with salt and pepper to taste, add cayenne if desired, and add cream. Stir to combine and heat through.

Garnish with fresh chives, cheddar cheese and/or oyster crackers if desired.

DUSTIN'S AWARD-WINNING CHILI

Dustin Sample - Madison Fire District

INGREDIENTS

2 pounds ground beef (or turkey)

2 packages mild chili seasoning

Small jar banana peppers, drained

1 jalapeño, diced small

1 small Vidalia sweet onion

1 can sweet corn, undrained

1 can black beans, undrained

1 tablespoon garlic, diced

1 can petite diced tomatoes, undrained

1 can large diced tomatoes, undrained

1 large can tomato paste

2 large cans tomato sauce

1 can light kidney beans, undrained

1 can dark kidney beans, undrained

½ cup sugar

¼ cup hot sauce (red hot)

Salt and pepper to taste

DIRECTIONS

Cook meat with onion, salt and pepper.

Add remaining ingredients into a slow cooker on low heat.

Add meat to slow cooker, stir, cover, cook on low for 4 hours.

Workrite FIRE SERVICE

SLOW COOKER TACO SOUP

Danny McKinney – City of Clinton Fire Dept.

INGREDIENTS

One 16-ounce can pinto beans

One 16-ounce can white beans or
one 16-ounce) can kidney beans

One 11-ounce can niblet corn

One 11-ounce can Rotel® tomatoes
and chilies

One 28-ounce can diced tomatoes

One 4-ounce can diced green chilies

One 1¼-ounce envelope taco seasoning
mix

One 1-ounce envelope Hidden Valley®
Original Ranch Dressing and Seasoning
Mix

1 pound of shredded chicken, ground
beef or 1 pound of any meat

DIRECTIONS

Cook meat and drain.

Shred if needed.

Add all ingredients to crock pot -
DO NOT DRAIN CANS.

Stir.

Cook on high for 2 hours or low for
4 hours.

Keep on low until serving to keep hot.

Garnish with sour cream, shredded
cheese, chopped green onions and/or
tortilla chips.

INGREDIENTS

1 large russet potato per firefighter

1 large carrot per firefighter

2 stalks of celery per firefighter

¼ yellow onion per firefighter

½ pounds chuck steak per firefighter

32-ounces of chicken stock

3 bay leaves

1 teaspoon peppercorn

Salt and ground black pepper

All-purpose flour

1-pound bag frozen peas

Olive or vegetable oil

PRESSURE COOKER BEEF STEW

Jim Kadeg - Dry Creek Rancheria Fire Dept.

DIRECTIONS

Cube steak into 1-inch chunks and season with salt and pepper. Then coat with flour.

Brown all meat in small batches, browning at least two minutes per side, in a large pan or pressure cooker.

Cut potatoes into quarters.

Cut carrots into 1½-inch pieces.

Cut celery into 1-inch pieces.

Cut onion into quarters.

Add meat, celery, carrots and onion into pressure cooker and mix ingredients.

Add peppercorns, 1 tablespoon of flour and bay leaves on top of ingredients in pressure cooker.

Add chicken stock up to 1-inch below ingredients in cooker.

Close cooker.

Put on steam release valve and cook on high heat until steam valve activates.

Reduce heat to medium or high enough to keep steam valve activated.

Cook for ½ an hour.

Turn off heat and let pressure reduce naturally as it cools.

Once steam valve has stopped hissing, remove valve and allow residual pressure to subside.

Open cooker, gently mix in peas, remove bay leaves and season with salt and pepper to taste.

Serve in a large "family"-style bowl with serving spoon.

Suggest sour cream for garnishing potatoes and a good crusty baguette or Italian bread with butter.

Start to finish: 1 hour.

We feed 4 at a time from each pot made.

BREAKFAST

Cheesy Egg Toast

Breakfast Burrito

CHEESY EGG TOAST
Alex Krechowics - Toronto Fire Services

INGREDIENTS

Sliced bread

Eggs

Shredded cheese

DIRECTIONS

Squish the center of a piece of sliced bread.

Put an egg in the center area.

Surround yolk with shredded cheese and bake at 400 F for about 10 minutes.

For an extra extra kick top with a soft poached egg.

BREAKFAST BURRITO
Joseph Honn - Ely Fire Dept.

INGREDIENTS

1 stick of Mexican chorizo

18 large, grade A eggs

4 cups of cheddar cheese

Large jar of your favorite salsa

24 flour tortillas

DIRECTIONS

Place tortillas in oven on low or room temperature.

Fry the chorizo in a small saucepan (cook well on medium heat, contains pork).

Scramble all the eggs in a medium-large saucepan until fluffy and desired texture.

Combine chorizo and eggs, keep warm.

Place tortillas on a plate, add chorizo/egg mixture, add cheese, add salsa and enjoy!

ENTRÉES

Baby Back Ribs

Vegetarian Pizza

"The Rock's" Chimichurri
Chicken

Balsamic Pork Chops

Gaucho-Style Steak with
Argentinian Chimichurri Sauce

Bacon Ranch Chicken

Pork Ribs

Al Pastor

Tamale Casserole

Bacon Wrapped Chicken Strips

Shrimp And Scallops in Wine
Sauce

Cheesy Chicken Roll Ups

Authentic Pad Thai

Berdan's BBQ Chicken

Chicken Parmesan

Chicken Rice Casserole

Verde Enchiladas and Rice

Jalapeño Macaroni and Cheese

Chicken and Dumplings

Mushroom Wine Chicken

Chile Chicken and Beans

Shrimp Boil

Deer Philly Cheese Steak Sandwich

Spaghetti Casserole

Chicken Bombs

Mexican Pasta Bake

Curry Chicken

Chicken and Sausage Pasta

BABY BACK RIBS

John Peurifoy - City of Riverside Fire Dept.

INGREDIENTS

Rack of ribs

Hot sauce

Yellow mustard

Spice rub

BBQ sauce

DIRECTIONS

Pull the skin from the back of the ribs.

Splash hot sauce over the ribs.

Apply a small amount of mustard on the ribs.

Using your hands, spread the hot sauce and mustard all over.

Sprinkle your favorite rub on the ribs. Using your hands rub it in really well.

Turn the ribs over and do the same to the front of the ribs.

Once the ribs have been coated, cover with plastic wrap or foil and place in the fridge for at least 4 hours. Better if over night.

Using any type of smoker, heat it to 225 F. (Hickory and cherrywood works great.)

Smoke the ribs for 3 hours.

Coat the ribs with your favorite BBQ sauce and put back in the smoker for 1 hour uncovered.

After the hour, remove from the smoker.

Wrap with foil tight. Place a towel over the ribs and let sit for 45 minutes and they will be tender and delicious.

VEGETARIAN PIZZA

Jason Chavez - Calfire

INGREDIENTS

1 cup of flour

1 large egg

Finely minced rosemary, mixed into dough

½ cup of tomato sauce

Freshly grated mozzarella

Small sweet peppers

2-3 cloves of garlic

¼ onion, sliced

DIRECTIONS

As dough sits to room temperature:

Sauté garlic, onion and peppers in a sauce pan. Cook until onions are transparent and peppers are slightly charred.

Roll out rested dough. Sauce with tomato sauce and grate fresh mozzarella over the top. Add grilled onions and peppers. Set oven to 425 F and bake for 21 minutes.

Adjust your waistband to allow for expansion.

"THE ROCK'S" CHIMICHURRI CHICKEN

Anthony Morganti - Los Alamitos Joint Forces Training Bases

INGREDIENTS

1 rack of boneless skinless chicken breasts

2 bushels of cilantro

1 habañero pepper

1 serrano pepper

6 limes, freshly squeezed

1½ cups soy sauce

8-inch piece of ginger root, peeled

1 red onion

1 cup olive oil

4 cloves of garlic

DIRECTIONS

Place all of the items (except chicken) in a food processor/blender until puréed.

Place chicken in large bowl and pour the marinade over and let sit for 30 minutes.

BBQ the chicken and baste during cooking. Serve over rice or in tortillas.

BALSAMIC PORK CHOPS

Joshua Jones - Frederick County Fire and Rescue Dept.

INGREDIENTS

8 boneless pork chops

½ teaspoon salt

¼ teaspoon black pepper

1 tablespoon olive oil

½ diced red onion

⅔ cup balsamic vinaigrette

¼ brown sugar

DIRECTIONS

Pat pork chops dry with paper towel.

Sprinkle salt and pepper on both sides of pork chops.

Heat oil in non stick skillet, on medium to high heat.

Cook pork chops for 4 minutes then flip to other side for 3 minutes.

Once pork chops are cooked, move to plate and keep warm.

Turn heat to high and add onions to pan and cook for 1 minute.

Put balsamic vinaigrette and brown sugar in skillet and cook for another minute.

Pour over pork chops and serve.

GAUCHO-STYLE STEAK
WITH ARGENTINIAN CHIMICHURRI SAUCE

John Wymore - Barstow Fire Protection District

INGREDIENTS

Argentinian Chimichurri Sauce:

1 cup lightly packed chopped parsley
(ideally flat leaf "Italian" parsley)

3 to 5 cloves garlic, minced

1 teaspoon salt

½ teaspoon freshly ground pepper

½ teaspoon chili pepper flakes

2 tablespoons fresh oregano leaves (optional)

2 tablespoons shallot or onion, minced

¾ cup vegetable or olive oil

3 tablespoons sherry wine vinegar, or red wine vinegar

3 tablespoons lemon juice

Steak:

1 tablespoon cayenne pepper

3 tablespoons salt

2½ pounds of rib-eye, New York strip, or sirloin steak, (about 1½-inch thick)

2 baguettes, sliced into ¼-inch thick slices

DIRECTIONS

Preheat a grill.

Place all chimichurri sauce ingredients in a blender or food processor and pulse until well chopped, but not puréed. Reserve.

Dissolve cayenne pepper and salt in 1 cup of hot water. Transfer to a squeeze container.

Place the steak directly over a hot grill, baste with the chimichurri grilling sauce and grill until the outer portion of the meat reaches the desired degree of doneness.

Remove the steak from the grill and slice long strips from the outer edges of the steak.

Instruct guests to pick up a steak slice from the cutting board with their fingers, place it on a slice of baguette and enjoy.

Return the remaining steak to the grill, baste and grill until more of the steak is cooked.

Remove and repeat the slicing and serving procedure until steak is consumed.

For extra spicy steak, baste 2 or 3 additional times with the cayenne pepper mixture during grilling process.

Spoon chimichurri sauce over steak. (Also brilliant on any grilled fish or chicken.)

Recommended beverage: Argentinian Malbec.

BACON RANCH CHICKEN

Jamal George - Midland Fire Dept.

INGREDIENTS

2-3 pounds boneless chicken breasts

Two 8-ounce blocks cream cheese

Two 1-ounce packets dry Ranch seasoning

8 ounces of bacon, cooked crisply and crumbled

DIRECTIONS

In a slow cooker combine chicken, cream cheese and Ranch seasoning.

Cook on low for 6-8 hours or on high for 4 hours, until chicken shreds easily.

Once chicken shreds, stir with a large fork or spoon, so the chicken shreds and all the ingredients combine.

Add in crumbled bacon and stir to incorporate.

Serve warm.

Serves 6.

ASIAN-STYLE PORK RIBS

Roger William - Taisacan Commonwealth Ports Authority,
Benjamin Taisacan Manglona International Airport

INGREDIENTS

1 slab of pork spare ribs

¼ cup of apple cider vinegar

¾ cup of Kikkoman® soy sauce

1 teaspoon of black pepper

2 teaspoon of Ajinomoto

2 clove of garlic, diced

DIRECTIONS

Combine ingredients and marinate ribs overnight before barbecue, allowing all ingredients to soak in.

Prep in a separate bowl 1 teaspoon of cayenne pepper with 1 squeeze of lemon, ¼ cup of Kikkoman® soy sauce and 1 diced clove of garlic for dipping to spice it up before eating.

AL PASTOR

Brian Hermo - Chester Fire Dept.

INGREDIENTS

5 pounds boneless pork shoulder

3 tablespoons smoked paprika

2 tablespoons ancho chili powder

1 tablespoon chipotle chile powder

1 tablespoon garlic powder

1 tablespoon oregano

1 tablespoon cumin

1 tablespoon salt

1 tablespoon pepper

½ cup white vinegar

1 cup pineapple juice

1 pineapple, skinned and sliced into 1-inch rounds

1 thick wooden skewer, trimmed to the height of your oven

10-12 small corn tortillas

1 white onion, chopped finely

1 cup cilantro, chopped finely

1 cup salsa of your choice

DIRECTIONS

Preheat oven to 350 F. Also works great on a smoker!!

Slice the pork shoulder into about 1-centimeter slices, then transfer to a large dish or bowl.

In a bowl, combine the smoked paprika, ancho chili powder, chipotle chili powder, garlic powder, oregano, cumin, salt, pepper, vinegar, and pineapple juice, mashing and stirring until smooth with no lumps.

Pour the marinade over the pork, then toss the pork slices to make sure that they are all coated on all sides. Wrap the dish/bowl in cling film, then marinate the pork for at least 2 hours, up to 3-5 days in the refrigerator.

On a baking sheet lined with parchment paper or foil, place a slice or two of the pineapple. Take a wooden skewer and push it directly in the middle of the pineapple.

Remove the pork from the fridge and push the slices through the skewer, layering one after the other until there is a 1-inch gap at the top. Push another pineapple slice on top.

Bake for about an hour and a half, until slightly charred on the outside and deep red.

Rest the meat for about 10 minutes, then carve off thin slices of the pork. Slice off thin pieces of the roasted pineapples as well.

To assemble and serve, place some pork on the tortillas, followed by a few pieces of pineapple, a sprinkle of onions, a pinch of cilantro and a small spoonful of the salsa.

Serves 10-12.

TAMALE CASSEROLE
Tini Franklin - La County Fire Dept.

INGREDIENTS

7 pounds ground beef

6 medium onions, chopped

2 celery ribs, chopped

3 garlic cloves, minced

Two 14-ounce cans diced tomatoes, undrained

Two 12-ounce cans tomato paste

Two 15¼-ounce cans whole kernel corn, drained

Two 4½-ounce cans mushroom stems and pieces, drained

Three 2¼-ounce cans sliced ripe olives, drained

2¼ to 2¾ cups water

2-3 tablespoons chili powder

1 tablespoon seasoned salt

½ to 1 teaspoon crushed red pepper flakes

1 teaspoon pepper

Three 12-ounce jars tamales, papers removed and halved

2 cups (8 ounces) shredded cheddar cheese

DIRECTIONS

In several Dutch ovens, cook the beef, onions, celery and garlic until meat is no longer pink; drain.

Stir in tomatoes and tomato paste.

Add the corn, mushrooms and olives.

Stir in water and seasonings.

Bring to boil, remove from heat.

Spoon into 3 greased 13 x 9 x 2-inch baking dishes.

Top with the tamales.

Cover and bake at 350 F for 50-60 minutes.

Sprinkle with cheese.

Bake 5 to 10 minutes longer or until cheese is melted.

Yields 3 casseroles (8 to 10 servings each).

BACON WRAPPED CHICKEN STRIPS

Tim Bailey - New Albany Fire Dept.

INGREDIENTS

Boneless chicken

Chili powder

Bacon

Brown sugar

DIRECTIONS

Cut boneless chicken breasts into strips.

Season chicken strips with a light coat of mild chili powder.

Wrap the seasoned chicken breast with a piece of bacon.

Then roll the bacon-wrapped chicken in light brown sugar.

Grill on medium to low-heat with water standing by for flare ups.

SHRIMP AND SCALLOPS IN WINE SAUCE

Mike Kazar - Selkirk Fire Dept.

INGREDIENTS

3 pounds medium shrimp

3 pounds bay scallops

4 tablespoons butter

½ cup cornstarch

4-6 cups milk

1½ cups white wine

6 cups cooked white rice

DIRECTIONS

Cook shrimp and scallops until done, set aside.

Slowly melt butter in saucepan.

Add cornstarch, then milk, stirring constantly.

Add wine, shrimp and scallops.

Serve over cooked rice.

CHEESY CHICKEN ROLL UPS
Rich Gluth Williams Bay – Wisconsin Fire Dept.

INGREDIENTS

9 x 12-inch baking pan

1 package skinless, boneless chicken breasts

1 large can and 1 regular size can cream of chicken soup

Milk

1 large package shredded cheddar cheese

2 large packages of crescent rolls

1 small package of crescent rolls

DIRECTIONS

Cut and cube the raw chicken into small pieces. (Suggestion: put them in the freezer for a while until they are about to freeze which makes it easier to cut.)

On the stovetop thoroughly cook the cubed chicken in butter, salt and pepper.

Once the chicken is cooked, you can begin the process of assembling.

Begin by placing 1 crescent roll flat. Put a finger full of chicken and a finger full of cheddar cheese at the end of the crescent roll. Beginning at the end with the chicken and cheese, roll up the crescent roll. Place the rolled crescent roll in a non-greased pan and continue this process for each crescent roll.

Place any extra cheese or chicken in the baking pan so that at the end you can scoop it up when serving the meal.

Empty the large can and 1 regular size can of cream of chicken soup into a mixing bowl and then fill each can about half full of milk. Add the milk and mix thoroughly. The sauce will be a little on the thicker side, which is what you want.

Pour the sauce over the roll ups, making sure you have enough sauce to cover the bottom of the pan but not so much that they are drowning in sauce.

Spread a layer of cheddar cheese over the top.

Bake at 350 F until they are golden brown.

Serves 6.

Serve with: any kind of rice like Chicken Rice-a-Roni® and a vegetable of choice.

AUTHENTIC PAD THAI RECIPE

Chris Lohan - Sioux Falls Fire Rescue

INGREDIENTS

1 box pad thai style rice noodles

1 jar pad thai sauce

1 pound chicken, cubed

1 pound shrimp, peeled and coarsely chopped

4 eggs

2 small yellow onions, thinly sliced

2 cups fresh mung bean sprouts (may substitute with canned)

1-2 bunches of green onion, chopped

1 bunch cilantro, chopped

1 tablespoon soy sauce

½ cup chopped nuts (we used cashews, though peanuts are traditional)

DIRECTIONS

Prepare noodles according to instructions on package and set aside.

Sauté onions until brown. Set aside in large mixing bowl.

Sauté chicken with soy sauce. When chicken is partially cooked, add shrimp and 1 cup of mung bean sprouts.

Remove all ingredients from pan and add to large mixing bowl with the sautéed onions. Scramble eggs and add to mixing bowl.

Add noodles, green onions, remaining cup of mung bean sprouts and sauce. Stir until ingredients are well combined. Add cilantro and nuts to garnish.

BERDAN'S BBQ CHICKEN

Chuck Berdan - Alameda County Fire Dept.

INGREDIENTS

2½ cups salad oil

2 cups sauternes wine

½ cup apple cider vinegar

1 cup chopped parsley

1 cup chopped
green onion

4 dashes Worcestershire® sauce

1 teaspoon garlic powder

1 teaspoon onion powder

Juice from ½ lemon

1 bay leaf, crushed

½ teaspoon Italian seasoning

3 pounds chicken pieces (your choice
of chicken parts - breast, thigh, wings,
legs or combination of all)

DIRECTIONS

Combine marinade ingredients in a
large bowl.

Place chicken in marinade and place
in refrigerator for 2 hours.

Preheat BBQ on medium high heat.

Remove chicken from marinade and
place on BBQ. Reserve marinade.

Brown all sides of the chicken
(approximately 25 minutes).

Layer the chicken in a Dutch oven.

Pour enough of the marinade in the Dutch
oven to cover chicken and cover with lid.

Place Dutch oven on BBQ and cook
30 minutes or until chicken is done.

Remove chicken from the Dutch oven
and place on a platter and serve.

CHICKEN PARMESAN
Sam Pascua - West Jordan Fire Dept.

INGREDIENTS

Chicken breasts

Flour (enough to coat chicken)

Eggs (enough to coat chicken)

1 box Panko® bread crumbs

Vegetable oil

Spaghetti sauce

Mozzarella/parmesan cheese
(enough to top chicken)

1 box noodles (any kind)

DIRECTIONS

Set oven to 450 F

Take chicken breast, cover in flour, then egg, then Panko®. Set aside.

Heat oil in a skillet. Once hot, take individual chicken breasts and fry in oil until Panko® turns dark brown.

Set all finished chicken breasts in baking dish. Cover breasts in spaghetti sauce and cheese.

Bake at 450 F for 15-20 minutes. Top with more cheese.

While chicken is baking, boil noodles. Once finished, drain and rinse. Add spaghetti sauce, cheese and butter to noodles. Simmer until warm and serve with chicken!

CHICKEN RICE CASSEROLE
Janis Elias - Volunteer Fire Fighter

INGREDIENTS

6 boneless chicken breasts, chunked

1 onion, diced

1 can each cream of mushroom, cream of chicken and cream of celery soups

1 cup jasmine rice

½ cup milk

1 stick butter, melted

Salt and pepper to taste

DIRECTIONS

Mix all ingredients together in a glass casserole dish and cover with foil.

Bake at 275 F for 2½ hours.

VERDE ENCHILADAS AND RICE
Marci Thoie - City of Duluth Fire Dept.

INGREDIENTS

Chicken (approximately ¼ pound per person, 1.5 pounds per pan)

Chicken broth (1 cup per pan)

Salsa verde (1 jar per pan)

Flour tortillas (2 per person, 10 fit in a pan)

Shredded pepper jack cheese
(3 cups per pan)

Basmati rice

Avocados (1 per every 4 servings)

Cilantro (as desired)

Lime juice (as desired)

Marinade (amounts are per pan):

½ cup honey

½ cup lime juice

1 tablespoon chili powder

1 teaspoon onion powder

1 teaspoon garlic powder

½ teaspoon smoked paprika

½ teaspoon salt

½ teaspoon chipotle powder

¼ teaspoon black pepper

DIRECTIONS

Heat a dash of oil in a skillet, then add chicken to brown on both sides.

Add the cup of broth, cover and reduce heat to medium until chicken is cooked through.

Remove chicken to cool slightly before shredding.

Stir together all marinade ingredients and add the shredded chicken to it.

Grease a baking pan and pour a little salsa on the bottom.

Toast tortillas slightly over the gas range.

Add two cups of the cheese to the chicken and mix well.

Fill tortillas evenly with chicken and cheese (black beans and corn are a nice addition as well), roll, and place in pan with seam side down.

Add remaining salsa and cheese on top before baking.

Bake at 350 F for at least 40 minutes.

While enchiladas are baking, rinse rice and cook in the rice cooker. Use chicken broth instead of water for cooking if you still have some left.

Mash avocados with a little lime juice and desired amount of cilantro.

When rice is done, stir in avocado mixture and serve it along side the enchiladas.

Garnish with remaining cilantro.

JALAPEÑO MACARONI AND CHEESE

Chris Parietti - Gales Ferry Fire Company

INGREDIENTS

8 ounces elbow macaroni
(½ box, 2 cup measure)

½ stick butter (4 tablespoons)

One onion, diced

½ cup flour

3 cups whole milk

1 teaspoon salt

¼ teaspoon black pepper

½ pound sharp cheddar, diced

4 slices real American cheese
(¼ pound), diced

2-4 tablespoons pickled jalapeños,
diced small

½ cup parmesan cheese, grated

DIRECTIONS

Boil macaroni 6-8 minutes
or as box directs, then drain
and set aside.

*Meanwhile, in a very large
saucepan:*

Heat onion and butter until
onion softens (approximately
7 minutes).

Stir in flour and cook 2 more
minutes.

Slowly add milk, 1 cup at a
time, stirring constantly to
break up lumps.

Add salt and pepper.

Simmer and stir until
sauce thickens and boils
(approximately 10 minutes).

Add cheddar and American
cheese, stir until melted.

Turn off heat and stir in
jalapeños.

Add macaroni and mix well
(so the sauce fills the pasta).

Pour into buttered baking
pan, 9-inch square or similar.

Sprinkle parmesan cheese
across top.

At this point it will freeze or
refrigerate well until needed.

To serve, bake at 375 F for
30 minutes or until parmesan
melts and browns to form
a crust.

CHICKEN & DUMPLINGS

Rick Pavick - Texarkana Arkansas Fire Dept.

INGREDIENTS

1 whole chicken cut into pieces

Pepper (to taste)

Garlic (to taste)

Paprika (to taste)

Seasoning salt (to taste)

Minced onion (to taste)

2 cups flour

1 teaspoon salt

1 teaspoon baking powder

2 tablespoons Crisco®

1 cup milk

DIRECTIONS

Boil and debone chicken, save broth.

Add pepper, garlic, paprika, touch of seasoning salt and minced onion to broth according to taste.

In a mixing bowl, combine flour, salt, baking powder, Crisco® and milk. Mix well to form a stiff dough.

Roll out dough as thin as you can and cut into squares.

Drop the dumpling squares into boiling broth for about 15 minutes, stirring often.

Add chicken back to the broth and serve.

MUSHROOM WINE CHICKEN

Josh Garcia – Clements Fire Dept.

INGREDIENTS

4 chicken breasts

1 box chopped mushrooms

1 tablespoon butter

1 cup white wine

¼ teaspoon thyme

¼ teaspoon parsley

4 garlic cloves

1 cup flour

2 teaspoons oil

DIRECTIONS

Flour chicken and brown in oil in a frying pan.

Place the chicken in a casserole dish.

Drain the excess oil and in the same pan, add sliced mushrooms, butter, white wine, thyme and parsley and simmer for 15 minutes.

Pour over chicken and cover. Bake at 350 F for 1 hour and remove cover for the last 15 minutes.

Serve with rice.

CHILE CHICKEN AND BEANS

Ken McGowan – San Diego County Fire

INGREDIENTS

4 boneless, skinless, chicken breasts, boiled and cut into cubes

1 medium yellow onion, chopped

3 teaspoons garlic powder

2 tablespoons vegetable oil

Four 15-ounce cans great northern beans, rinsed and drained

Four 15-ounce cans low sodium chicken broth

Three 4-ounce cans chopped green chilies (2 mild, 1 hot)

2 teaspoons salt

2 teaspoons ground cumin

2 teaspoons dried oregano

2 teaspoons black pepper

½ teaspoon cayenne pepper

2 cups sour cream

1 cup whipping cream

DIRECTIONS

In large saucepan, sauté chicken, onion and garlic powder in oil.

Add beans, broth, chilies and seasonings.

Bring to boil.

Reduce heat and simmer uncovered for 30 minutes, stirring occasionally.

Remove from heat and stir in sour cream and whipping cream.

Let sit for 15 minutes until sauce thickens.

Serve immediately or pour into a crock pot on warm.

SHRIMP BOIL

Damien Furtman- Kirtland Air Force Base Fire Dept.

INGREDIENTS

8 cups water

One 12-16 ounce bottle of beer (optional)

½ cup Old Bay® Seasoning

½ cup cajun seasoning (I use Joe's Hot Stuff® cajun seasoning from New Orleans School of Cooking)

¼ cup lemon pepper seasoning

1 lemon, halved

1 orange, halved

1 stick butter (optional)

1 clove garlic, cleaned up and top cut off

1 teaspoon salt

2 medium red potatoes, quartered

1 medium onion, cut into wedges

1 pound pre-cooked andouille sausage, cut into 2-inch pieces

2 ears fresh corn, shucked and halved

2 pounds ez-peel raw jumbo shrimp

Lemon wedges for serving

DIRECTIONS

Bring water, beer, Old Bay®, cajun seasoning, butter, lemon, garlic and salt to a rolling boil in large stockpot on high heat.

Add potatoes and onions. Cook 8 minutes.

Add smoked sausage. Cook 5 minutes.

Add corn. Cook 7 minutes.

Stir in shrimp. Cook 3-4 minutes or just until shrimp turn pink.

Drain and reserve broth for dipping.

Pour food into large serving bowl, platter or mound on paper-covered table.

Sprinkle with additional Old Bay® seasoning.

If desired, serve with lemon wedges.

DEER PHILLY CHEESE STEAK SANDWICH

Jerry Copeny - Chattanooga Fire Dept.

INGREDIENTS

1 pound deer steak, sliced thin

Dale's Seasoning®

Onion powder

Garlic powder

Salt

Black pepper

Day old bread from Jimmy John's®

Onion

Bell peppers

Peanut oil

Cheese Whiz®

DIRECTIONS

Wash meat under running water until no blood remains and slice thinly.

Marinate in Dales Seasoning®, onion powder, garlic powder, light salt and pepper. (About 2 hours or longer)

Sauté onions and peppers in peanut oil uncovered until they glaze and are broken down. Then lightly salt and pepper.

After meat marinade process is done, use same pan used for onion/pepper sautée to cook meat until tender. Add a ¼ cup of Cheese Whiz®. Stir in until evenly mixed in.

(I used cast iron and covered the pan at times on and off in order to introduce steam so the meat would not be dry.)

Take Jimmy John's® loaf and cut in half. Slice each half down the middle. Spoon or cut out half of the middle to give you an opportunity to taste the other ingredients better

Place meat on bottom bun, sprinkle on onions and peppers, then add a line of Cheese Whiz® on top of sandwich contents. Then put top on and microwave for 10 seconds.

SPAGHETTI CASSEROLE

Stockton Trujillo – Ogden City Fire Dept.

INGREDIENTS

2 pounds ground beef

¼ cup chopped onion

Two 21.5-ounce cans of meatless spaghetti sauce

One 16-ounce container fat-free sour cream

2 cups shredded mozzarella cheese, divided

½ cup parmesan cheese

Salt and black pepper to taste

Package of spaghetti noodles

DIRECTIONS

Preheat oven to 350 F degrees.

Grease a deep 9 x 13-inch baking dish.

Bring a large pot of salted water to a boil over high heat. Stir in the spaghetti.

Boil the pasta until cooked through but still firm to the bite, 8 to 10 minutes. Drain well.

Brown ground beef and onion in a large skillet over high heat; drain fat.

Stir in the spaghetti sauce, sour cream, and 1 cup of the mozzarella.

Mix in the cooked pasta.

Transfer pasta mixture to prepared baking dish.

Top with remaining 1 cup of mozzarella and the parmesan cheese.

Cover pan with aluminum foil.

Bake in preheated oven until hot and bubbly, about 30 minutes.

CHICKEN BOMBS

Justin Barker – Rockwall Fire Dept.

INGREDIENTS

1 package of chicken tenders

Whole jalapeños (each jalapeño makes 2 bombs)

Cream cheese

Bacon (1 strip per bomb)

DIRECTIONS

Beat the chicken down to make them thinner and season with any dry rub you like.

Cut the jalapeños in half scoop out the seeds and wash the jalapeños in water.

Fill the halved jalapeños with cream cheese, wrap a piece of chicken around the jalapeño then wrap with a piece of bacon and place a tooth pick in the middle to hold in place.

Place wrapped chicken bombs on a baking sheet bake for approximately 20 minutes at 375 F in the oven.

After 20 minutes take them out of the oven and off the baking sheet.

Place them on the grill at low heat for approximately 20 minutes and you're done!

MEXICAN PASTA BAKE

Cathy Werner – Gouldsboro Volunteer Fire Co.

INGREDIENTS

3 pounds 80% ground beef

3 pounds wide egg noodles

3 packets dry taco seasoning

4 large cans small diced tomatoes

2 jars salsa sauce

3 pounds fine shredded Colby cheese

DIRECTIONS

Boil the noodles until tender, drain but do not rinse.

Lightly brown the ground beef, add the seasoning, tomatoes and salsa.

In a very large oven container, combine the beef mixture with the cooked noodles and cheese

Bake 30 minutes at 350 F.

Serve with a green salad, bread and butter.

CURRY CHICKEN

Chris Adlington – Blue Island Fire Dept.

INGREDIENTS

Thighs and breast from 2 chickens bone-in with skin removed.

One large onion, chopped

One green pepper, chopped

McCormick® curry powder to taste. At least three tablespoons. Mild, hot, or a mix.

4 tablespoons flour

4 tablespoons olive oil

2 cups chicken broth

8 ounces tomato paste

DIRECTIONS

Coat chicken with curry. Brown in olive oil. Remove and set aside.

Brown vegetables in oil. Add flour and brown lightly.

Add additional curry powder to taste. Sauté a bit.

Add the chicken stock and tomato paste. Cook until moderately thick.

Adjust salt and pepper, as desired.

Pour sauce over chicken in a baking dish, cover with foil and bake at 350 F until done, about 40 minutes.

Uncover the last 15 minutes, basting every 5 minutes.

Serve with basmati rice and naan bread.

CHICKEN & SAUSAGE PASTA

Brad Kwatcher – Bellingham Fire Dept.

INGREDIENTS

1 pound bow tie pasta

1 pound chicken breasts, cubed

1 pound bulk Italian sausage*, hot or sweet

1 pint grape tomatoes

3 cloves garlic, minced

1 jar sun-dried tomatoes

1 bag spinach

1 box low sodium chicken stock

4-5 tablespoons olive oil

1 pinch (or more depending on desired heat level) crushed red pepper

Kosher salt and freshly ground pepper to taste

Bulk sausage is sausage out of the casing and ground. If you cannot find it, just use regular sausage, however remove the casing.

DIRECTIONS

Bring a pot of salted water to a boil, cook pasta to desired texture.

While water is coming to a boil, cook sausage until cooked through, drain and set aside.

Add cubed chicken to the pan with more olive oil and some of the reserve fat from sausage. Season with salt and pepper. Once chicken is golden and brown, take it out of the pan, and set aside.

If needed, add olive oil to pan, add grape tomatoes, and cook 2-3 minutes.

Add garlic and cook until fragrant (don't burn it!).

Add sun-dried tomatoes and cook for another 2-3 minutes.

Add spinach. Season with salt and pepper.

Once the spinach has wilted down, add chicken and sausage back to the pan. If the mixture is dry, add some of the chicken stock (there is usually enough liquid from the spinach to bring the sauce together).

Cook until chicken is cooked through. Season as needed.

Once all combined, add pasta to the pan and toss to combine with a good helping of parmesan cheese.

Variations: If making for a bigger crowd, just double the amounts. For example, for every 1 pound of pasta, add another pound of sausage and chicken, add another pint of tomatoes, more garlic, two bags of spinach, etc.

DESSERTS

Triple-Decker Strawberry Cake

Buttermilk Pie

Lemon Meringue Pie

Apple Crisp

Carrot Cake

TRIPLE-DECKER STRAWBERRY CAKE

William Smith - Texarkana Arkansas Fire Dept.

INGREDIENTS

One 18.25-ounce package white cake mix

One 3-ounce package strawberry gelatin

4 large eggs

½ cup sugar

¼ cup all-purpose flour

½ cup finely chopped fresh strawberries

1 cup vegetable oil

½ cup milk

Strawberry Buttercream Frosting

1 cup butter, softened

Two 17-ounce packages powdered sugar, sifted

1 cup finely chopped fresh strawberries

DIRECTIONS

Beat the cake mix and next 7 ingredients at low speed with an electric mixer for 1 minute.

Scrape down the sides and beat at medium speed 2 more minutes, stopping to scrape down sides, if needed. (Strawberries should be well blended into batter.)

Pour batter into 3 greased and floured 9-inch cake pans.

Bake at 350 F for 23 minutes.

Cool in pans on wire racks for 10 minutes.

Remove from pans; cool completely on wire racks.

ICING DIRECTIONS

Combine butter and sugar until mixed well. Add strawberries and stir until they are well incorporated.

BUTTERMILK PIE

Stephen Johnson -
Texarkana Arkansas Fire Dept.

INGREDIENTS

3 eggs

1½ cups sugar

1 cup buttermilk

2 tablespoons all-purpose flour

1 teaspoon vanilla extract

1 stick butter, melted and cooled

Pie shell, unbaked

DIRECTIONS

Combine sugar, flour & butter.

Add 3 eggs, one at a time, beating each time.

Add vanilla.

Beat in buttermilk.

Pour into unbaked pie shell.

Bake at 300 F for 10 minutes, then reduce oven to 250 F and bake 30-45 minutes until set and light brown.

LEMON MERINGUE PIE

Greg Garcia - Clements Fire District

INGREDIENTS

One 9-inch ready-to-bake pie crust

⅓ cup corn starch

⅛ teaspoon salt

1½ cups sugar

½ cup lemon juice

4 eggs, separated

1 tablespoon butter

¼ teaspoon cream of tarter

1½ cups water

DIRECTIONS

Bake pie crust.

In a sauce pan stir in corn starch, salt, 1 cup of sugar, water and lemon juice.

Stir over medium heat until lemon mixture is thickened and starts to boil then remove from heat.

In a small bowl whisk egg yolks, then scoop in a little bit of the hot mixture and pour back into the pot of lemon mixture.

Return to heat and stir constantly until lemon mixture thickens, do not boil.

Stir in the butter, pour into the pie crust and cool for 10 minutes.

Preheat oven to 400 F.

In a small bowl, beat the egg whites and cream of tarter until soft peaks form.

Gradually stir in ½ cup of sugar; the whites should stand in stiff peaks.

Put the meringue on the pie and bake for 10 minutes or until the peaks on top of the pie are golden brown.

CARROT CAKE

Dale Barnett - Cal Fire

INGREDIENTS

2 cups white sugar

3 eggs

1 ¼ cups oil

1 teaspoon salt

2 teaspoons cinnamon

1 small can crushed pineapple

1 cup coconut flakes

3 cups grated carrot (about 4 long carrots)

½ cup chopped walnuts

2 teaspoons baking soda

1 teaspoon vanilla

2¼ cups flour

Frosting:

1 pound powdered sugar

One 8-ounce package of cream cheese, softened

2 teaspoons vanilla

1 cube butter, softened

DIRECTIONS

Preheat oven to 350 F.

Grease and flour 9 x 13-inch glass pan (use butter to grease, not oil).

Mix white sugar, eggs and oil together.

Add in salt, cinnamon, pineapple, coconut flakes, carrot, walnuts, baking soda, 1 teaspoon vanilla and flour.

Dump mixture into prepared pan.

Bake for approximately 48 minutes, or when middle comes out 'almost' clean with a toothpick (do not overbake).

Let cool prior to frosting.

Mix frosting ingredients together and spread over cooled cake.

Cover and refrigerate at least 8 hours. It's always better the next day.

APPLE CRISP
Antonia Bello - Gold Ridge Fire Dept.

INGREDIENTS

9 x 13-inch pan

8 large apples sliced (Gravenstein or Granny Smith)

2 teaspoons cinnamon

¾ cup sugar

½ cup flour

½ teaspoon salt

A little lemon juice

Topping:

1 cup flour

1 cup sugar

1 egg

1 stick (½ cup) butter

DIRECTIONS

Preheat oven to 350 F.

Peel and slice the apples to ¼-inch thickness.

Put apple slices in a large bowl.

Drizzle 1 tablespoon of lemon juice over the apples to prevent them from turning brown and toss.

In a separate bowl mix the cinnamon, sugar and salt together. Combine this with the apple slices.

Toss until all the slices are coated.

Sprinkle the flour over the mixture, tossing again to coat. The flour helps absorb some of the juice and liquid from the mixture.

Transfer the apple mixture to a greased 9 x 13-inch baking pan.

For the topping, beat one egg in a medium size bowl and combine the flour and sugar.

Using a fork, mix the ingredients together until it creates a crumble topping. Do not over mix.

There will be some dry ingredients in the bottom of the mixture. Spread the mixture over the top of the apples.

Melt 1 stick of butter and pour over the topping.

Bake for 40 minutes uncovered.

Side note: I double the topping and it is extra delicious...ENJOY!

WHY FR STATION WEAR?

HIDDEN HAZARDS

Firefighters understand the dangers of heat and flame better than anyone, yet many of them are not protected against these dangers as well as they could — and should — be.

Firefighter turnout gear is designed specifically to provide protection against heat and flame. But what about the station wear underneath?

While turnout gear covers station wear, certain emergency situations may expose this clothing to heat or flame. If exposed, non-FR station wear can further endanger the wearer. For instance, 100 percent cotton station wear can become completely consumed by flames. Polycotton fabrics are even worse — they can both burn and melt, greatly multiplying damage to the skin. FR uniforms not only won't melt but they also maintain their appearance better and last 2 to 3 times longer than polycotton or cotton which actually saves money over time. This can help improve public perception and department morale.

100% COTTON

POLYCOTTON

FR FABRIC

WITHSTAND THE HEAT

After exposure to fire, Workrite's flame-resistant station wear quickly self-extinguishes and polycotton both burns and melts.

COMPLETE PROTECTION

Like turnout gear, FR station wear does not ignite and continue to burn or melt when exposed to heat or flame. This provides an added layer of protection that increases your chances of minimizing injuries.

No standard mandates the use of FR station wear, but it seems like common sense — wear clothing that maximizes your chances of survival in dangerous situations. Period.

For more information about our flame-resistant station wear, call **1-800-521-1888**, email **info@workrite.com** or visit **fireservicefr.com**

Workrite® FRx
FIRE SERVICE

COOKBOOK

★ FIRE SERVICE ★
VOL. 2
RECIPES FROM FIREFIGHTERS

For more information about our flame-resistant station wear,
call 1-**800-521-1888**, email **info@workrite.com** or visit **fireservicefr.com**

Made in United States
Orlando, FL
18 April 2022

16935561R10040